This Jo... Belongs to:

Awesome Principal

TEACHER FIRST,

Principal

SECOND.

Behind every great school is a caring Principal.

Ideas of How to Use This Journal:

- Write down funny things that your students or teachers say

- Use this journal for your own reflection and diarizing.

- Take this journal on a trip in the summer to record your adventures.

It takes a
BIG HEART
to shape
little minds

THANK YOU FOR
MAKING ME
one smart
COOKIE

TEACHER

Nutritional Facts

Serving Size: 1 Awesome Teacher*

Amount Per Serving: 1 Full Classroom	
	%Daily Value**
Hard Working	1000%
Determination	150%
Passion	500%
Caring	300%
Regret	0%
Caffeine	110%

* Not a Significant Source of Fear.
** Percent Daily Values are Based on Your Unique Diet.

Extra
ordinary
educator

Coffee: Because *awesome* *teachers* can't live *on apples* alone!

A GOAL IS

Dream

WITH a

DEADLINE

IF

YOU

NEVER TRY

YOU'LL

Never

KNOW

Teachers PLANT SEEDS THAT GROW forever

★ **Teachers are** ☽
〉 *like unicorns* 〈
★ **they make** ☾
magic happen

Educator of Tiny humans

COFFEE
gives me
TEACHER
POWER

TODAY I LEAD THE SCHOOL.

Tomorrow my students will

lead the world.

Never underestimate the value of a great Principal in the life of a child.

Thank you for everything that you do!

Made in the USA
Coppell, TX
26 May 2023

17334100R00066